THE STORY OF
THE
CONSTITUTION

Tamra Orr

Mitchell Lane
PUBLISHERS

P.O. Box 196
Hockessin, Delaware 19707

My Guide to the
CONSTITUTION

THE BILL OF RIGHTS
THE EXECUTIVE BRANCH
THE JUDICIAL BRANCH
THE LEGISLATIVE BRANCH
THE POWER OF THE STATES
THE STORY OF THE CONSTITUTION

Copyright © 2012 by Mitchell Lane Publishers

Printing   1   2   3   4   5   6   7   8   9

PUBLISHER'S NOTE: The Constitution of the United States appears in the appendix to this book. The amendments to the Constitution, including the Bill of Rights, appear in the appendix to My Guide to the Constitution: *The Bill of Rights.*

The facts on which the story in this book is based have been thoroughly researched. Documentation of such research can be found on page 45. While every possible effort has been made to ensure accuracy, the publisher will not assume liability for damages caused by inaccuracies in the data, and makes no warranty on the accuracy of the information contained herein.

**Library of Congress
Cataloging-in-Publication Data**
Orr, Tamra.
    The story of the Constitution / by Tamra Orr.
        p. cm.—(My guide to the Constitution)
    Includes bibliographical references and index.
    ISBN 978-1-58415-946-9 (library bound)
    1. United States. Constitution—Juvenile literature. 2. United States—Politics and government—1775–1783—Juvenile literature. 3. United States—Politics and government—1783–1789—Juvenile literature.
    I. Title.
    E303.O77 2011
    973.3—dc22
                                                                  2011002747

Paperback ISBN: 9781612281889
eBook ISBN: 9781612280905

                                                                        PLB

CONTENTS

Words in bold type can be found in the glossary.

Chapter 1

Calling a Convention

George Washington sat back in his hard wooden chair and sighed. He listened to the crackling of the fire and gratefully soaked up its warmth. He could easily remember when he had been utterly cold and miserable. Those long, brutal days at Valley Forge, eighteen miles outside of Philadelphia, had almost been the end of him. He had watched as thousands of his men struggled against starvation and freezing weather. Those who managed to survive hunger, cold, and disease stood and fought when they had to—they'd paid dearly for the country's freedom.

Washington wanted to make sure he honored the war's veterans by continuing to fight to protect that hard-won freedom. So much had been accomplished already—the war was over, a new nation had been born—but there was plenty more to do. It was not enough for the nation to exist. It needed a government to run it fairly and honestly.

Gilbert Stuart's painting
of George Washington, 1797

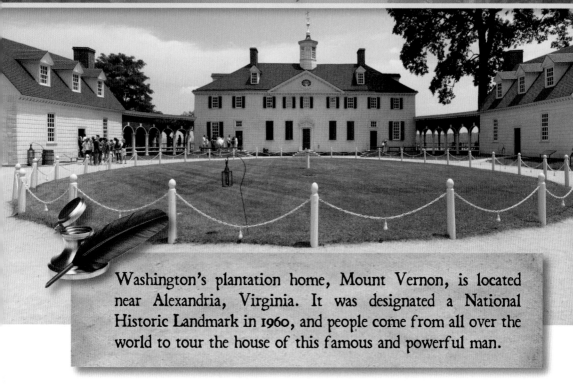

Washington's plantation home, Mount Vernon, is located near Alexandria, Virginia. It was designated a National Historic Landmark in 1960, and people come from all over the world to tour the house of this famous and powerful man.

The one that had been established right after the war, the Articles of Confederation, was proving to be inadequate.

He shook his head. He knew the country needed help, but he was not sure what role he could play. He had already hosted one meeting at his home at Mount Vernon two years before, in 1785. Men from several states had come to talk about problems with the Articles of Confederation and it had gone quite well. Now it was time for another meeting, but a much larger one, with all the states represented.

Time for a Revolution

In 1775, determined men and women had joined together to escape from British rule. They were tired of having no control over their lives. The British **monarchy** controlled everything. Laws were made and taxes imposed, and the colonists had no legal way to protest or refuse them. Basic freedoms such as speech and religion were squashed under the king's strict rule. These people had had enough. It was time to fight back. They started the Revolutionary War.

By July 1776, while the war raged on, a newly formed Congress had issued the official Declaration of Independence. Written largely by Thomas Jefferson over the course of two and a half weeks, it created a new United States that was completely separate from the British Empire.

George Washington had been the general in that war for freedom, and he was delighted when the thirteen colonies had become the United States. However, his worries were far from over. How would this new nation be governed? How would it stay united? What kind of leadership would it have? How much power should be given to those leaders? He did not know the answers to these questions. He only knew that no one wanted this new nation to be anything like the one they had just sacrificed so much to leave.

The Articles of Confederation

Washington was not the only one with these questions and concerns. Everyone who had fought to escape British rule wanted to make sure they would never experience the same kind of **tyranny** again.

The group of men who had formed the country's Continental Congress gathered again. They had written the Declaration of Independence a year before. Now it was time to put pen to paper once more. This time, the team, made up of half a dozen representatives, wrote the Articles of Confederation. This document called for all thirteen states to establish a "firm league of friendship." Congress would be made up of people from each of the thirteen states and would be responsible for dealing with foreign countries, declaring war or peace, and maintaining a working army. However, that was the end of the government's power. Each state was allowed to decide the rest. Collecting taxes and enforcing laws, for example, would be under the power of each individual state.

Congress adopted the Articles of Confederation in November 1777. It went into official operation in March 1781, after the last of the thirteen states agreed to its rules and signed the document.

Full of Problems

For years, the Articles of Confederation remained in place. As time passed, the colonies grew—and grew. By 1787, almost four million people lived throughout the new country. Cities were born, and each one differed from the others. Businesses and trade items changed from one state to another. People's religious beliefs varied. Even local customs and attitudes shifted from one place to the next. These differences began to create conflicts and arguments. It became more and more clear that the Articles of Confederation, although a great start, was not thorough enough to cope with the growing nation. The document contained basic rules but no real punishment for not following them—so why should people do so? For example, if Congress

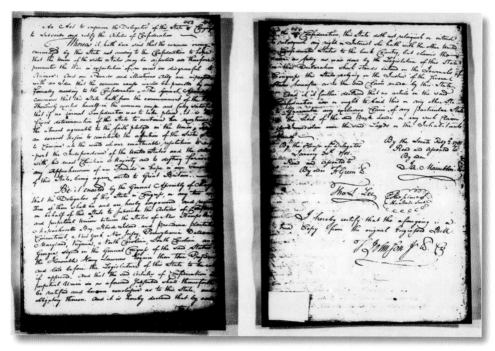

Act of Maryland to Ratify the Articles. When the Maryland legislature ratified the Articles of Confederation in 1781, the country finally became united—but this was not enough. More guidance was needed for the new nation.

stated that it needed money, the states were not required to provide it. It was their choice. Congress could declare war, but it was up to each state whether or not to send any soldiers. What was legal in one state might be illegal in another. Which laws did a person follow if he was traveling? Who enforced the punishment for breaking a law? The confusion just kept mounting.

People in some states began to argue with people from others. Fighting broke out over some issues, and it was clear that big trouble was brewing. Finally, Washington, along with his friends Alexander Hamilton and James Madison, decided that something had to be done. It was time to call another meeting.

The three men asked each state to send delegates to Philadelphia, Pennsylvania, one of the largest and most developed cities in the country. Washington was excited about the idea—finally, everyone would gather and discuss the Articles of Confederation and how they needed to change. They would discuss and debate them, patch any holes, polish them, and then add a few new ideas. Soon the document would be new and improved—and therefore, so would the nation.

Rising from his chair by the fire, Washington smiled. Although he had planned to stay home and relax for a few months, he knew he had bigger plans now. He could not wait to get to the convention. He had helped form this new nation, and now he would help strengthen and unite it.

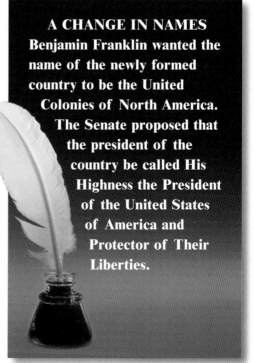

A CHANGE IN NAMES
Benjamin Franklin wanted the name of the newly formed country to be the United Colonies of North America. The Senate proposed that the president of the country be called His Highness the President of the United States of America and Protector of Their Liberties.

Chapter 2

Meeting the Framers

The word spread. **Delegates** from each of the thirteen states were invited to the upcoming convention in the State House (now called Independence Hall) in Philadelphia. Although some people were just as eager as Washington to make the trip—and make some changes—others were not so sure this was the right choice. Some of them did not feel the Articles of Confederation needed to be changed. Others thought meeting about it would just make things worse.

The state of Rhode Island refused to send anyone at all—it was the only state not represented. Rhode Island was worried that, as the smallest of the states, it would lose too many rights and too much power if the Articles were changed. Patrick Henry, a delegate from Virginia, said, "No thanks, I'm not going." He told others that he "smelt a rat." Willie Jones, the delegate from North Carolina, agreed with Henry. He would not be making the trip either.

The National Constitution Center in Philadelphia is devoted to telling the history of the Constitution and exploring what it means today.

The official starting date for the convention was May 14, 1787. The hall's doors were opened and it was time to begin—but James Madison realized there was a problem. Discussions could not start until at least seven states were represented. On May 14, there were only two! It took another eleven days before enough delegates had arrived to start the meeting.

Why had they been late? Some blamed it on bad weather and muddy roads. Others had struggled to raise the money to make the trip. Although a total of 73 delegates were invited, 55 were at the convention, and most of the time, the hall had only about 30 in attendance.

Famous Framers

James Madison looked around the hall. At last, everyone seemed ready to get started.

From the beginning, Madison had been the main planner of the event. He had helped organize the delegates, and during the proceedings, he would sit in the front row taking long and detailed notes of every speech, vote, and discussion. He would spend every night changing his quick notes and shorthand into the only records ever kept of this history-changing event. He never missed a day.

Madison glanced over at Washington. He was not at all surprised that Washington had been unanimously elected president of the convention right away. After all, he had been an excellent commander of the Continental Army. For most of the meeting, Washington was a quiet but powerful force. At six feet tall, he towered over many of the other delegates. Perhaps this was part of how he kept the meetings orderly—not an easy chore when many men were passionate about their points of view. Unlike many of the other delegates, Washington spoke only once, and that was near the end of the convention. The leadership he showed during the convention helped the delegates decide to elect him as the first president of the United States.

What was that noise? Madison looked up. Of course—it was the convention's oldest and loudest delegate, Benjamin Franklin. At eighty-one years old, Franklin's health would not allow him to walk to Independence Hall. Instead, he had arrived at the convention carried on a portable chair by four inmates from the nearby prison. Franklin was an amazing storyteller, and after one of his speeches at the convention, delegate William Pierce stated, "He is, however, a most extraordinary Man, and tells a story in a style more engaging than anything I ever heard."

Gouverneur Morris, a representative from Pennsylvania, was another talented communicator. He gave more speeches than any other delegate and was responsible for writing several important parts of the Constitution's final draft. Pierce stated, "No Man has more wit, nor can anyone engage the attention more than Mr. Morris." Morris had been in the original group of men who signed the Articles of Confederation.

Alexander Hamilton was the delegate from New York. Although he missed a good portion of the convention, he was there to debate the different plans and to put his signature on the final draft.

Jonathan Dayton

On May 25, 1787, the Constitutional Convention officially began. It would last for almost four months. The delegates ranged in age from Jonathan Dayton, the youngest at 26, to Franklin's 81. Over half of them had graduated from college, many of them from Yale and Harvard. The majority of them had some kind of background in law, government, or both. All of them were white and male. Most were somewhat wealthy. Although they all had a great deal in common, they also had different ideas of what their new nation needed and how to get it. Now was the time to examine those points of view.

Setting the Rules

Once enough delegates had arrived, the convention started. Nothing could get done, however, until some rules were put into place. These rules were:

1. At least seven states had to be represented in order for any meeting to be held.
2. All decisions would be made through majority vote. Each state was given one vote.
3. The purpose of the meeting was to revise the Articles of Confederation.
4. No official records were to be kept in order to keep the meeting secret. Only Madison's notes were permitted.

Once these rules were established, the talking started. It did not take long before it was quite clear that rule number three would have to be changed. There were far too many problems and conflicts between the states to simply revise the Articles. Instead, an entirely new document was called for. It soon became known as "the plan."

Powerful Decisions

For the next four months, the men in this room would argue and debate ideas. They would propose plans—and reject them. They would weigh issues and make decisions. All of them were sobered by the knowledge that the choices they made would not only affect themselves but all of the people who lived in the states—and those still to come. Creating a constitution—a "supreme law of a country" that controls the functions and powers of the government—was an enormous chore. It could not be taken lightly. All of these men knew what kind of government they did not want. They had learned those lessons from Great Britain.

Despite all the debating, the men at the convention agreed on some of the basics. The nation had to be built on the idea of personal liberty and individual freedom for every single person. It had to offer its people the right to speak and worship freely without fear of punishment. It also had to clearly define what powers and rights the government had, and which ones it did not. Living in a country where the leaders had all the power had taught these men that it was not what they wanted for their new home. Figuring out exactly what type of government they wanted was the next challenge.

ACCEPTING A BET

Alexander Hamilton had an idea. He bet delegate Gouverneur Morris that Morris would not have the courage to walk up and slap Washington on the back. In their day, it was not an accepted gesture—especially to someone as respected as Washington. Morris took the challenge. He walked up to Washington and put his hand on his shoulder. Washington said nothing—he just looked at Morris. Morris later reported that he had tried to sink through the floor but failed.

Chapter 3

Keeping It Secret

Washington carefully opened his coat. Franklin used his notes for a fan. Madison paused in his writing to wipe the sweat from his forehead. As the temperatures soared outside, so did the discomfort inside Independence Hall. Summer in Philadelphia in 1787 brought unusually hot weather, and the delegates were miserable.

Hamilton looked out the closest window. How he wished he could just walk over and push aside the curtain and throw the window open. He closed his eyes and imagined the breeze that would begin blowing through the hall. He could almost feel it sweeping past him. He sighed. Unfortunately, that was not going to happen. The meeting was supposed to be kept as secret as possible. The doors and windows had to stay closed and the curtains drawn. As the day wore on, the room grew hotter.

The delegates also had another problem—flies! The heat and sweat attracted them. Once they flew

Independence Hall

into the hall, they had no way to escape. They buzzed and pestered the men constantly.

Staying Quiet

Although the people of Philadelphia certainly knew that dozens of important men had traveled to their city that summer, those in the other states were not aware of the gathering. The delegates wanted it this way. They needed time to talk and make decisions without pressure from people asking questions about what was going on. Even the newspapers did not know what was happening. There were no reporters waiting at the doors to get the latest scoop.

To help make sure the meeting would remain secret, each member took an oath not to discuss it with anyone outside. Although the men were allowed to write letters back home to their families, they had to keep them vague—no details of what was happening or who was there could be divulged. The only member who really had trouble staying quiet was Benjamin Franklin. He loved to be the center of attention and tell great stories to interested audiences. It was extremely difficult for him not to talk about what he was doing every day. Finally, another delegate was assigned to follow Franklin to any parties or dinners he attended. Whenever Franklin would start to reveal something secret, this delegate stepped in and changed the topic of conversation.

Sentries were placed at all the doors of the hall, and only those who were invited to the convention were allowed in or out. Because of this high level of secrecy, except for Madison's notes, there are no formal records of what went on. (William Jackson, Washington's secretary, also took notes at the convention. These were destroyed when the Constitution was signed.)

The secrecy left room for rumors to fly as people tried to guess what was going on behind the closed doors. Some people thought the men were planning to bring in someone from the British monarchy to help them govern. Others were sure the men were creating an all-new kind of government and feared it would not be a fair or popular one.

Luther Martin was one of the people who refused to sign the Constitution. He worried that it was too powerful and would interfere with the individual states' rights.

Taking Time to Listen

Washington tried not to show his impatience. It was not easy. For weeks, the men had been talking and talking. Everyone had important points to make—well, except for Luther Martin, the representative from Maryland. The man loved to hear himself talk and he did so—often and loudly. He frequently repeated himself, speaking for over three hours at a time, and Washington had to admit the information was not that interesting even the first time. He glanced around the room whenever Martin spoke. He smiled when he spotted Franklin napping through the speech. Even Madison put down his pen for a little while.

There were so many issues to talk about—and so many points of view to consider. As the weeks turned into months, discussions often

A Florida wax museum helps visitors imagine some of the nation's founding fathers. From left to right are Patrick Henry, Benjamin Franklin, Alexander Hamilton, Nathan Hale, Thomas Jefferson (seated, center), George Washington, John Adams, and James Madison.

turned into debates. Debates turned into arguments. Some of the delegates feared the convention would come to a close without any real agreement or progress to show for it. Washington wrote a letter to Hamilton in mid-July in which he explained his frustration. "I almost despair of seeing a favorable issue to the proceedings of the Convention," he wrote.

At one time, Franklin stood up and suggested that each meeting should be opened with a prayer to encourage peace and good will. The idea was quickly dismissed. Who would pay for someone to come in and deliver a prayer? And wouldn't that just start more rumors?

One of the biggest conflicts was between the smaller states and the larger ones. The smaller states were worried, understandably, that they would have less power than the larger states. They wanted every state to have equal **representation** within the government, regardless of the state's population. The larger states disagreed. At one point, the smaller states even began to threaten that, if not given equal representation, they would form treaties with foreign countries. It was an empty threat—but it showed how desperate some of them were feeling.

A number of other issues were upsetting people. How much power should the government have? What rights should remain with the states? Who should be the head of the government? What limitations should he have? How long should his term be? Should he be paid? What about the issue of slavery? Some states wanted to keep the practice and others wanted it abolished.

It was clear that the convention needed to answer some large questions before an actual constitution could be written. Thanks to the hardworking delegates, that is just what happened next.

SHH! MEN WORKING
To help make sure the men could hear clearly, the people of Philadelphia covered the cobblestone streets in front of Independence Hall with gravel. The gravel muffled the sound of horses' hooves and carriage wheels.

Chapter 4

Making Tough Decisions

Madison put down his quill and stretched his fingers. They were long past tired and cramped. Keeping up with everyone's speeches and decisions was a tough job. He felt like he spent every minute of his life writing. From his notetaking in the sessions to his rewrites done by candlelight at night, he was constantly scribbling.

Virginia v. New Jersey

As he wrote, Madison listened carefully to everyone's arguments. Today, he was taking notes on a plan proposed by Edmund Randolph, the governor of Virginia. Randolph was a likable fellow, easy to talk to, but when he had stood up and outlined a new plan, he had created quite a furor. He was suggesting a federal government that was made up of three branches. The executive branch, he suggested, would be in charge of running the government. The legislative branch would be divided into two houses and would create the laws. The judicial branch would

James Madison,
by John Vanderlyn, 1816

include a Supreme Court that would be responsible for enforcing laws and punishing those who did not follow them.

When Randolph explained that, with this "Virginia Plan," the representatives in the legislature would be based on population, delegates from the smaller states began to clamor. When he further pointed out that this new government would have national power over the states, more voices erupted in anger. Men stood up and yelled. They threw up their hands and slapped the tables. Clearly, Randolph's idea was not fully supported.

One of the people who did not like this new plan was William Paterson, the delegate from New Jersey. He had a different idea. His "New Jersey" plan also included the same three branches of government.

Many of the framers would have important roles in the new government. Washington (left) became president. In his cabinet were Secretary of War Henry Knox, Secretary of Treasury Alexander Hamilton, Secretary of State Thomas Jefferson, and Attorney General Edmund Randolph.

However, it would have one house in the legislature, and every state would have only one vote, regardless of population. This time, delegates from the larger states protested. The issue was further complicated by the question of slavery. If power was based on population, did slaves count? If they did, what would stop a state from buying more slaves just to increase its population and voting power?

For weeks, these two plans were debated. Neither side was willing to admit defeat. Some delegates were so upset, they threatened to walk out of the whole convention. The situation was getting desperate. That was when Roger Sherman, the delegate from Connecticut, came up with a new idea. Although it was called the Connecticut Plan at first, it soon became known as the Great Compromise.

The Great Compromise
The Great Compromise combined the Virginia and New Jersey plans. It stated:

1. There would be three branches of government.
2. The legislative branch would have two houses, or be **bicameral.**
3. The Senate would have two representatives from each state, regardless of size.
4. The House of Representatives would have one representative for every 30,000 people who lived in that state.
5. Slaves would count as three-fifths a person (every five slaves counted as three people).

Although pleasing everyone was impossible, this plan pleased enough of the delegates that they passed it. Finally, there was progress!

A List of Issues
At last, a plan had been approved—but the work was far from over. One of the biggest issues that had to be decided was slavery. Could it continue? Were the southern states willing to sign a constitution that

An American Slave Market, painted in 1852. The right to buy and keep slaves was one of the most debated issues of the convention. The difference of opinions between the North and the South would spark the Civil War many years later.

didn't allow for slavery? The delegates decided that the South could keep importing slaves until 1808—another 20 years. They also said that no state was allowed to stop a runaway slave from being returned to his or her owner.

Another issue was **trade regulation.** Should the national government have the power to decide what could be traded? Could it tax those items, such as rice and tobacco? The men voted to allow Congress to regulate interstate trade (trade between the states), but not intrastate trade (trade within each state) or trade with foreign countries. **Exports** could not be taxed, but **imports** could be.

Other topics that were decided include

- How the president should be elected (each state would be given the same number of electoral votes as they had representatives)
- How to divide the power between national and state governments
- What checks and balances needed to be in place so that none of the branches became too powerful
- How **amendments (changes)** could be made to the Constitution

Now that a compromise had been reached and the major issues had been decided, it was time to do what all the delegates had been waiting for: take a break! For ten days the men relaxed and spent time with their wives and children. They wandered around the city seeing shows, eating at restaurants, and going to parties. George Washington went trout fishing in Valley Forge.

After the men returned, relaxed and renewed, they continued to debate and discuss. They decided how many states would have to agree to the Constitution in order for it to be ratified, or legally accepted. They decided on nine of the thirteen. Finally, on September 15, the Constitution was sent to a committee to be formally written out. Two days later, the parchment returned. The convention was almost over—but there were still a few important steps to take.

ALMS FOR THE POOR?
Independence Hall was located close to a four-story stone prison. Whenever the delegates would come outside to take a break, the prisoners would thrust long sticks at them with cloth purses on the end. These "begging sticks" were used to ask for money from passersby. If people didn't give, the prisoners would yell and boo at them.

Chapter 5

Signing the Constitution

Madison watched the doubt wash over the delegates' faces. He had worried that there would be some last-minute hesitations, and he had been right. Seeing the **resolutions** written on paper made people start to wonder if they had made the right decisions. Discussing them for hours was one thing. Putting their signatures on a formal document was something else entirely. Three of the delegates got cold feet, changing their minds at the last minute. Edmund Randolph, Elbridge Gerry, and George Mason all refused to sign the Constitution.

Randolph, who thought the plan differed too much from the Virginia Plan, wanted to wait and see what the people of his state thought about the document. Gerry was worried that the Constitution did not represent the people, that the executive branch would have too much power, and that it would encourage war among the states. Mason thought the government would become a monarchy

Scene at the Signing of the Constitution of the United States, by Howard Chandler Christy, 1940

Anti-Federalist George Mason, as painted by John Hesselius in 1750. In 1957, a branch of the University of Virginia was named George Mason University in his honor.

or a tyranny. He wanted more individual rights added to the document before he would sign it.

A number of delegates shared Mason's worry. They believed that since the Constitution left out the specific rights that they all knew were so important, it was incomplete. Where was the right to free speech? Where were the rights to free worship and to trial by jury?

In the end, 39 of the 55 delegates stood in line, picked up a quill, dipped it in ink, and signed one of the most important documents in history. Gouverneur Morris stated as the men gathered to leave, "The moment this plan goes forth, all other considerations will be laid aside—and the great question will be, shall there be a national government or not? And this must take place or a general **anarchy** will be the alternative."

Federalists and Anti-Federalists

The Constitutional Convention came to an official end on September 17, 1787. The delegates packed up their things and returned to their home states, taking a copy of the Constitution with them. It was their job to share the document with the people in their state and get their approval. Only then could it finally be **ratified.**

Before long, the people who were in favor of the Constitution were being called **Federalists.** Those with concerns or objections were known as **Anti-Federalists.** The Federalists were led largely by James Madison, John Jay, and Alexander Hamilton. They wrote a total of 85 letters to New York newspapers explaining the many reasons why ratifying the Constitution was the right decision to make. Each letter was written under the pen name of Publius.

At the same time, a handful of Anti-Federalists, led by Patrick Henry, Elbridge Gerry, and George Mason, also wrote letters urging the states not to ratify the Constitution. Many of those letters appeared under the pen name Cato. These men firmly believed that the document would

The Federalist Papers were originally published in three different New York newspapers. From the three writers, there were often three or four new essays appearing in print every week under the name of Publius.

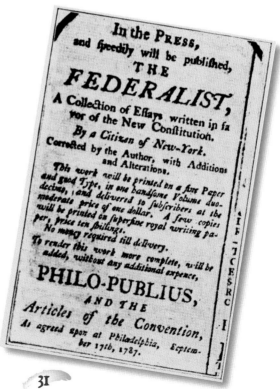

give the federal government too much power. Without some changes, they said, people's individual rights would not be protected. They urged people to insist that a Bill of Rights be added to the Constitution.

While the Federalist and Anti-Federalist letters were appearing in newspapers, each state was holding its own special convention to discuss the Constitution. It took six months for the states to organize and hold these gatherings. The meetings were usually full of controversy and arguments. Occasionally, the conflicts spilled over into fistfights, duels, and even riots.

At the Massachusetts ratification convention, one of the largest in the country, a farmer named Amos Singletary spoke out about his concern that the Constitution had been created by and would be controlled by only wealthy men. These were men who did not understand what it was like to struggle just to survive, he said, so how could they represent the country? Singletary stated at the convention, "These lawyers and men of learning, and moneyed men that talk so finely, and gloss over matters so smoothly, to make us poor illiterate people swallow down the pill, expect to get into Congress themselves. They expect to be the managers of this Constitution, and get all the power and all the money into their own hands. And then they will swallow up all us little folks . . . just as the whale swallowed up Jonah."

Time for Ratification

On December 7, 1787, Delaware became the first state to ratify the Constitution. It was followed in order by Pennsylvania, New Jersey, Georgia, Connecticut, Massachusetts, Maryland, South Carolina, and New Hampshire. These were enough for ratification, but they were followed by Virginia, New York, and North Carolina. On March 4, 1789, the Constitution of the United States finally went into effect. Rhode Island—the last to agree—signed in May 1790.

The country paused to celebrate. In Philadelphia, a huge parade called the Grand Federal Procession was held on the Fourth of July. It started at 9:30 a.m. and went until 6:00 p.m. At the head of the parade

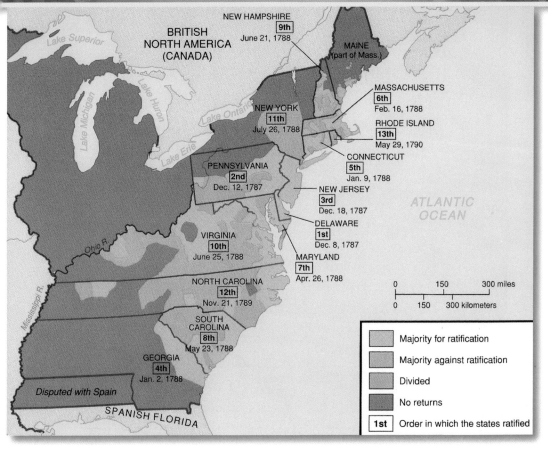

NEW HAMPSHIRE
9th
June 21, 1788

BRITISH
NORTH AMERICA
(CANADA)

MAINE
(part of Mass.)

MASSACHUSETTS
6th
Feb. 16, 1788

NEW YORK
11th
July 26, 1788

RHODE ISLAND
13th
May 29, 1790

CONNECTICUT
5th
Jan. 9, 1788

PENNSYLVANIA
2nd
Dec. 12, 1787

NEW JERSEY
3rd
Dec. 18, 1787

DELAWARE
1st
Dec. 8, 1787

VIRGINIA
10th
June 25, 1788

MARYLAND
7th
Apr. 26, 1788

NORTH CAROLINA
12th
Nov. 21, 1789

SOUTH
CAROLINA
8th
May 23, 1788

GEORGIA
4th
Jan. 2, 1788

ATLANTIC
OCEAN

Disputed with Spain

SPANISH FLORIDA

Lake Superior · Lake Michigan · Lake Huron · Lake Ontario · Lake Erie · Ohio R. · Mississippi R.

0	150	300 miles
0	150	300 kilometers

- Majority for ratification
- Majority against ratification
- Divided
- No returns

| 1st | Order in which the states ratified |

Two states did not ratify the Constitution until after it went into effect on March 4, 1789.

was a trumpeter, followed by riders on horseback. Next came floats and carriages pulled by horses. Lively, loud bands played music to keep everyone stepping in time. More than five thousand people marched down the street, including coopers and tailors, goldsmiths and bricklayers, bakers, printers, and gunsmiths. At the very end of the parade came the federal ship *Union*. It rode on a frame, along with twenty guns. When the parade ended, everyone was invited to a city picnic—and 17,000 people came!

Over the years, the Constitution of the United States has gone through a number of changes. Almost immediately, some of the delegates began writing the Bill of Rights, a set of amendments that addressed the concerns of the Anti-Federalists. Although the

The incredible assembly of the country's greatest political minds finished their work with their signatures, and their beliefs became the laws of the land.

amendments were narrowed down to ten, the states had sent in more than 200 proposals. These rights covered everything from the basic right to say and believe whatever a person wants without fear of punishment to the rights a person should have when accused of a crime. Other amendments focus on how rights are limited to what is listed in the Bill of Rights, and which powers belong to the state governments instead of to the federal government. The Bill of Rights was ratified on December 15, 1791.

Since 1791, only 17 other amendments have been added to the Constitution. Thousands of them have been proposed but very few are accepted by both houses of Congress and by the president. Some of them fail because they do not make much sense. For example, in 1933, an amendment was proposed to make it illegal for any person to be worth more than $1 million. In 2005, an amendment to do away with all taxes was proposed. The amendments that did pass include abolishing slavery (13th), prohibiting the sale of alcohol (18th) and then repealing that law (21st), and giving women the right to vote (19th).

SHORT BUT PRECISE
Although countless hours of thought, debate, discussion, and work went into creating the U.S. Constitution, it is only 4,543 words long (including all the delegates' signatures). That is the shortest constitution of any major government in the world.

When the 55 delegates gathered in Pennsylvania in 1787, they knew they had an important mission. Few may have realized just how monumental this meeting was, however. Instead of just revising the old rules, they hashed out new ones. It took months, tremendous effort, and a great deal of passion, but they did it. The document may not have been perfect, but it was an amazing achievement. More than 200 years later, people are still working to understand and analyze it. The Constitution formed the foundation of a new nation and continues to guide its people today.

Note: The following text is a transcription of the Constitution in its original form. Items that are in *italic* type have since been amended or superseded.

We the People of the United States, in Order to form a more perfect Union, establish Justice, insure domestic Tranquility, provide for the common defence, promote the general Welfare, and secure the Blessings of Liberty to ourselves and our Posterity, do ordain and establish this Constitution for the United States of America.

Article. I.

Section. 1. All legislative Powers herein granted shall be vested in a Congress of the United States, which shall consist of a Senate and House of Representatives.

Section. 2. The House of Representatives shall be composed of Members chosen every second Year by the People of the several States, and the Electors in each State shall have the Qualifications requisite for Electors of the most numerous Branch of the State Legislature.

No Person shall be a Representative who shall not have attained to the Age of twenty five Years, and been seven Years a Citizen of the United States, and who shall not, when elected, be an Inhabitant of that State in which he shall be chosen.

Representatives and direct Taxes shall be apportioned among the several States which may be included within this Union, according to their respective Numbers, which shall be determined by adding to the whole Number of free Persons, including those bound to Service for a Term of Years, and excluding Indians not taxed, three fifths of all other Persons. The actual Enumeration shall be made within three Years after the first Meeting of the Congress of the United States, and within every subsequent Term of ten Years, in such Manner as they shall by Law direct. The Number of Representatives shall not exceed one for every thirty Thousand, but each State shall have at Least one Representative; and until such enumeration shall be made, the State of New Hampshire shall be entitled to chuse three, Massachusetts eight, Rhode-Island and Providence Plantations one, Connecticut five, New-York six, New Jersey four, Pennsylvania eight, Delaware one, Maryland six, Virginia ten, North Carolina five, South Carolina five, and Georgia three.

When vacancies happen in the Representation from any State, the Executive Authority thereof shall issue Writs of Election to fill such Vacancies.

The House of Representatives shall chuse their Speaker and other Officers; and shall have the sole Power of Impeachment.

Section. 3. The Senate of the United States shall be composed of two Senators from each State, *chosen by the Legislature* thereof for six Years; and each Senator shall have one Vote.

Immediately after they shall be assembled in Consequence of the first Election, they shall be divided as equally as may be into three Classes. The Seats of the Senators of the first Class shall be vacated at the Expiration of the second Year, of the second Class at the Expiration of the fourth Year, and of the third Class at the Expiration of the sixth Year, so that one third may be chosen every second Year; *and if Vacancies happen by Resignation, or otherwise, during the Recess of the Legislature of any State, the Executive thereof may make temporary Appointments until the next Meeting of the Legislature, which shall then fill such Vacancies.*

No Person shall be a Senator who shall not have attained to the Age of thirty Years, and been nine Years a Citizen of the United States, and who shall not, when elected, be an Inhabitant of that State for which he shall be chosen.

The Vice President of the United States shall be President of the Senate, but shall have no Vote, unless they be equally divided.

The Senate shall chuse their other Officers, and also a President pro tempore, in the Absence of the Vice President, or when he shall exercise the Office of President of the United States.

The Senate shall have the sole Power to try all Impeachments. When sitting for that Purpose, they shall be on Oath or Affirmation. When the President of the United States is tried, the Chief Justice shall preside: And no Person shall be convicted without the Concurrence of two thirds of the Members present.

Judgment in Cases of Impeachment shall not extend further than to removal from Office, and disqualification to hold and enjoy any Office of honor, Trust or Profit under the United States: but the Party convicted shall nevertheless be liable and subject to Indictment, Trial, Judgment and Punishment, according to Law.

Section. 4. The Times, Places and Manner of holding Elections for Senators and Representatives, shall be prescribed in each State by the Legislature thereof; but the Congress may at any time by Law make or alter such Regulations, except as to the Places of chusing Senators.

The Congress shall assemble at least once in every Year, and such Meeting *shall be on the first Monday in December,* unless they shall by Law appoint a different Day.

Section. 5. Each House shall be the Judge of the Elections, Returns and Qualifications of its own Members, and a Majority of each shall constitute a Quorum to do Business; but a smaller Number may adjourn from day to day, and may be authorized to compel the Attendance of absent Members, in such Manner, and under such Penalties as each House may provide.

Each House may determine the Rules of its Proceedings, punish its Members for disorderly Behaviour, and, with the Concurrence of two thirds, expel a Member.

Each House shall keep a Journal of its Proceedings, and from time to time publish the same, excepting such Parts as may in their Judgment require Secrecy; and the Yeas and Nays of the Members of either House on any question shall, at the Desire of one fifth of those Present, be entered on the Journal.

Neither House, during the Session of Congress, shall, without the Consent of the other, adjourn for more than three days, nor to any other Place than that in which the two Houses shall be sitting.

Section. 6. The Senators and Representatives shall receive a Compensation for their Services, to be ascertained by Law, and paid out of the Treasury of the United States. They shall in all Cases, except Treason, Felony and Breach of the Peace, be privileged from Arrest during their Attendance at the Session of their respective Houses, and in going to and returning from the same; and for any Speech or Debate in either House, they shall not be questioned in any other Place.

No Senator or Representative shall, during the Time for which he was elected, be appointed to any civil Office under the Authority of the United States, which shall have been created, or the Emoluments whereof shall have been encreased during such time;

and no Person holding any Office under the United States, shall be a Member of either House during his Continuance in Office.

Section. 7. All Bills for raising Revenue shall originate in the House of Representatives; but the Senate may propose or concur with Amendments as on other Bills.

Every Bill which shall have passed the House of Representatives and the Senate, shall, before it become a Law, be presented to the President of the United States: If he approve he shall sign it, but if not he shall return it, with his Objections to that House in which it shall have originated, who shall enter the Objections at large on their Journal, and proceed to reconsider it. If after such Reconsideration two thirds of that House shall agree to pass the Bill, it shall be sent, together with the Objections, to the other House, by which it shall likewise be reconsidered, and if approved by two thirds of that House, it shall become a Law. But in all such Cases the Votes of both Houses shall be determined by yeas and Nays, and the Names of the Persons voting for and against the Bill shall be entered on the Journal of each House respectively. If any Bill shall not be returned by the President within ten Days (Sundays excepted) after it shall have been presented to him, the Same shall be a Law, in like Manner as if he had signed it, unless the Congress by their Adjournment prevent its Return, in which Case it shall not be a Law.

Every Order, Resolution, or Vote to which the Concurrence of the Senate and House of Representatives may be necessary (except on a question of Adjournment) shall be presented to the President of the United States; and before the Same shall take Effect, shall be approved by him, or being disapproved by him, shall be repassed by two thirds of the Senate and House of Representatives, according to the Rules and Limitations prescribed in the Case of a Bill.

Section. 8. The Congress shall have Power To lay and collect Taxes, Duties, Imposts and Excises, to pay the Debts and provide for the common Defence and general Welfare of the United States; but all Duties, Imposts and Excises shall be uniform throughout the United States;

To borrow Money on the credit of the United States;

To regulate Commerce with foreign Nations, and among the several States, and with the Indian Tribes;

To establish an uniform Rule of Naturalization, and uniform Laws on the subject of Bankruptcies throughout the United States;

To coin Money, regulate the Value thereof, and of foreign Coin, and fix the Standard of Weights and Measures;

To provide for the Punishment of counterfeiting the Securities and current Coin of the United States;

To establish Post Offices and post Roads;

To promote the Progress of Science and useful Arts, by securing for limited Times to Authors and Inventors the exclusive Right to their respective Writings and Discoveries;

To constitute Tribunals inferior to the supreme Court;

To define and punish Piracies and Felonies committed on the high Seas, and Offences against the Law of Nations;

To declare War, grant Letters of Marque and Reprisal, and make Rules concerning Captures on Land and Water;

To raise and support Armies, but no Appropriation of Money to that Use shall be for a longer Term than two Years;

To provide and maintain a Navy;

To make Rules for the Government and Regulation of the land and naval Forces;

To provide for calling forth the Militia to execute the Laws of the Union, suppress Insurrections and repel Invasions;

To provide for organizing, arming, and disciplining, the Militia, and for governing such Part of them as may be employed in the Service of the United States, reserving to the States respectively, the Appointment of the Officers, and the Authority of training the Militia according to the discipline prescribed by Congress;

To exercise exclusive Legislation in all Cases whatsoever, over such District (not exceeding ten Miles square) as may, by Cession of particular States, and the Acceptance of Congress, become the Seat of the Government of the United States, and to exercise like Authority over all Places purchased by the Consent of the Legislature of the State in which the Same shall be, for the Erection of Forts, Magazines, Arsenals, dock-Yards, and other needful Buildings;--And

To make all Laws which shall be necessary and proper for carrying into Execution the foregoing Powers, and all other Powers vested by this Constitution in the Government of the United States, or in any Department or Officer thereof.

Section. 9. The Migration or Importation of such Persons as any of the States now existing shall think proper to admit, shall not be prohibited by the Congress prior to the Year one thousand eight hundred and eight, but a Tax or duty may be imposed on such Importation, not exceeding ten dollars for each Person.

The Privilege of the Writ of Habeas Corpus shall not be suspended, unless when in Cases of Rebellion or Invasion the public Safety may require it.

No Bill of Attainder or ex post facto Law shall be passed.

No Capitation, or other direct, Tax shall be laid, *unless in Proportion to the Census or enumeration herein before directed to be taken.*

No Tax or Duty shall be laid on Articles exported from any State.

No Preference shall be given by any Regulation of Commerce or Revenue to the Ports of one State over those of another; nor shall Vessels bound to, or from, one State, be obliged to enter, clear, or pay Duties in another.

No Money shall be drawn from the Treasury, but in Consequence of Appropriations made by Law; and a regular Statement and Account of the Receipts and Expenditures of all public Money shall be published from time to time.

No Title of Nobility shall be granted by the United States: And no Person holding any Office of Profit or Trust under them, shall, without the Consent of the Congress, accept of any present, Emolument, Office, or Title, of any kind whatever, from any King, Prince, or foreign State.

Section. 10. No State shall enter into any Treaty, Alliance, or Confederation; grant Letters of Marque and Reprisal; coin Money; emit Bills of Credit; make any Thing but gold and silver Coin a Tender in Payment of Debts; pass any Bill of Attainder, ex post facto Law, or Law impairing the Obligation of Contracts, or grant any Title of Nobility.

No State shall, without the Consent of the Congress, lay any Imposts or Duties on Imports or Exports, except what may be absolutely necessary for executing it's inspection Laws: and the net Produce of all Duties and Imposts, laid by any State on Imports or Exports, shall be for the Use of the Treasury of the United States; and all such Laws shall be subject to the Revision and Controul of the Congress.

No State shall, without the Consent of Congress, lay any Duty of Tonnage, keep Troops, or Ships of War in time of Peace, enter into any Agreement or Compact with another State, or with a foreign Power, or engage in War, unless actually invaded, or in such imminent Danger as will not admit of delay.

Article. II.

Section. 1. The executive Power shall be vested in a President of the United States of America. He shall hold his Office during the Term of four Years, and, together with the Vice President, chosen for the same Term, be elected, as follows:

Each State shall appoint, in such Manner as the Legislature thereof may direct, a Number of Electors, equal to the whole Number of Senators and Representatives to which the State may be entitled in the Congress: but no Senator or Representative, or Person holding an Office of Trust or Profit under the United States, shall be appointed an Elector.

The Electors shall meet in their respective States, and vote by Ballot for two Persons, of whom one at least shall not be an Inhabitant of the same State with themselves. And they shall make a List of all the Persons voted for, and of the Number of Votes for each; which List they shall sign and certify, and transmit sealed to the Seat of the Government of the United States, directed to the President of the Senate. The President of the Senate shall, in the Presence of the Senate and House of Representatives, open all the Certificates, and the Votes shall then be counted. The Person having the greatest Number of Votes shall be the President, if such Number be a Majority of the whole Number of Electors appointed; and if there be more than one who have such Majority, and have an equal Number of Votes, then the House of Representatives shall immediately chuse by Ballot one of them for President; and if no Person have a Majority, then from the five highest on the List the said House shall in like Manner chuse the President. But in chusing the President, the Votes shall be taken by States, the Representation from each State having one Vote; A quorum for this purpose shall consist of a Member or Members from two thirds of the States, and a Majority of all the States shall be necessary to a Choice. In every Case, after the Choice of the President, the Person having the greatest Number of Votes of the Electors shall be the Vice President. But if there should remain two or more who have equal Votes, the Senate shall chuse from them by Ballot the Vice President.

The Congress may determine the Time of chusing the Electors, and the Day on which they shall give their Votes; which Day shall be the same throughout the United States.

No Person except a natural born Citizen, or a Citizen of the United States, at the time of the Adoption of this Constitution, shall be eligible to the Office of President; neither shall any Person be eligible to that Office who shall not have attained to the Age of thirty five Years, and been fourteen Years a Resident within the United States.

In Case of the Removal of the President from Office, or of his Death, Resignation, or Inability to discharge the Powers and Duties of the said Office, the Same shall devolve on the Vice President, and the Congress may by Law provide for the Case of Removal, Death, Resignation or Inability, both of the President and Vice President, declaring what Officer shall then act as President, and such Officer shall act accordingly, until the Disability be removed, or a President shall be elected.

The President shall, at stated Times, receive for his Services, a Compensation, which shall neither be increased nor diminished during the Period for which he shall have been elected, and he shall not receive within that Period any other Emolument from the United States, or any of them.

Before he enter on the Execution of his Office, he shall take the following Oath or Affirmation:--"I do solemnly swear (or affirm) that I will faithfully execute the Office of President of the United States, and will to the best of my Ability, preserve, protect and defend the Constitution of the United States."

Section. 2. The President shall be Commander in Chief of the Army and Navy of the United States, and of the Militia of the several States, when called into the actual Service of the United States; he may require the Opinion, in writing, of the principal Officer in each of the executive Departments, upon any Subject relating to the Duties of their respective Offices, and he shall have Power to grant Reprieves and Pardons for Offences against the United States, except in Cases of Impeachment.

He shall have Power, by and with the Advice and Consent of the Senate, to make Treaties, provided two thirds of the Senators present concur; and he shall nominate, and by and with the Advice and Consent of the Senate, shall appoint Ambassadors, other public Ministers and Consuls, Judges of the supreme Court, and all other Officers of the United States, whose Appointments are not herein otherwise provided for, and which shall be established by Law: but the Congress may by Law vest the Appointment of such inferior Officers, as they think proper, in the President alone, in the Courts of Law, or in the Heads of Departments.

The President shall have Power to fill up all Vacancies that may happen during the Recess of the Senate, by granting Commissions which shall expire at the End of their next Session.

Section. 3. He shall from time to time give to the Congress Information of the State of the Union, and recommend to their Consideration such Measures as he shall judge necessary and expedient; he may, on extraordinary Occasions, convene both Houses, or either of them, and in Case of Disagreement between them, with Respect to the Time of Adjournment, he may adjourn them to such Time as he shall think proper; he shall receive Ambassadors and other public Ministers; he shall take Care that the Laws be faithfully executed, and shall Commission all the Officers of the United States.

Section. 4. The President, Vice President and all civil Officers of the United States, shall be removed from Office on Impeachment for, and Conviction of, Treason, Bribery, or other high Crimes and Misdemeanors.

Article. III.

Section. 1. The judicial Power of the United States shall be vested in one supreme Court, and in such inferior Courts as the Congress may from time to time ordain and establish. The Judges, both of the supreme and inferior Courts, shall hold their Offices during good Behaviour, and shall, at stated Times, receive for their Services a Compensation, which shall not be diminished during their Continuance in Office.

Section. 2. The judicial Power shall extend to all Cases, in Law and Equity, arising under this Constitution, the Laws of the United States, and Treaties made, or which shall be made, under their Authority;--to all Cases affecting Ambassadors, other public Ministers and Consuls;--to all Cases of admiralty and maritime Jurisdiction;--to Controversies to which the United States shall be a Party;--to Controversies between two or more States;--*between a State and Citizens of another State,*--between Citizens of different States,--between Citizens of the same State claiming Lands under Grants of different States, and between a State, or the Citizens thereof, and foreign States, Citizens or Subjects.

In all Cases affecting Ambassadors, other public Ministers and Consuls, and those in which a State shall be Party, the supreme Court shall have original Jurisdiction. In all the other Cases before mentioned, the supreme Court shall have appellate Jurisdiction, both as to Law and Fact, with such Exceptions, and under such Regulations as the Congress shall make.

The Trial of all Crimes, except in Cases of Impeachment, shall be by Jury; and such Trial shall be held in the State where the said Crimes shall have been committed; but when not committed within any State, the Trial shall be at such Place or Places as the Congress may by Law have directed.

Section. 3. Treason against the United States, shall consist only in levying War against them, or in adhering to their Enemies, giving them Aid and Comfort. No Person shall be convicted of Treason unless on the Testimony of two Witnesses to the same overt Act, or on Confession in open Court.

The Congress shall have Power to declare the Punishment of Treason, but no Attainder of Treason shall work Corruption of Blood, or Forfeiture except during the Life of the Person attainted.

Article. IV.

Section. 1. Full Faith and Credit shall be given in each State to the public Acts, Records, and judicial Proceedings of every other State. And the Congress may by general Laws prescribe the Manner in which such Acts, Records and Proceedings shall be proved, and the Effect thereof.

Section. 2. The Citizens of each State shall be entitled to all Privileges and Immunities of Citizens in the several States.

A Person charged in any State with Treason, Felony, or other Crime, who shall flee from Justice, and be found in another State, shall on Demand of the executive Authority of the State from which he fled, be delivered up, to be removed to the State having Jurisdiction of the Crime.

No Person held to Service or Labour in one State, under the Laws thereof, escaping into another, shall, in Consequence of any Law or Regulation therein, be discharged from such Service or Labour, but shall be delivered up on Claim of the Party to whom such Service or Labour may be due.

Section. 3. New States may be admitted by the Congress into this Union; but no new State shall be formed or erected within the Jurisdiction of any other State; nor any State be formed by the Junction of two or more States, or Parts of States, without the Consent of the Legislatures of the States concerned as well as of the Congress.

The Congress shall have Power to dispose of and make all needful Rules and Regulations respecting the Territory or other Property belonging to the United States; and nothing in this Constitution shall be so construed as to Prejudice any Claims of the United States, or of any particular State.

Section. 4. The United States shall guarantee to every State in this Union a Republican Form of Government, and shall protect each of them against Invasion; and on Application of the Legislature, or of the Executive (when the Legislature cannot be convened), against domestic Violence.

Article. V.

The Congress, whenever two thirds of both Houses shall deem it necessary, shall propose Amendments to this Constitution, or, on the Application of the Legislatures of two thirds of the several States, shall call a Convention for proposing Amendments, which, in either Case, shall be valid to all Intents and Purposes, as Part of this Constitution, when ratified by the Legislatures of three fourths of the several States, or by Conventions in three fourths thereof, as the one or the other Mode of Ratification may be proposed by the Congress; Provided that no Amendment which may be made prior to the Year One thousand eight hundred and eight shall in any Manner affect the first and fourth Clauses in the Ninth Section of the first Article; and that no State, without its Consent, shall be deprived of its equal Suffrage in the Senate.

Article. VI.

All Debts contracted and Engagements entered into, before the Adoption of this Constitution, shall be as valid against the United States under this Constitution, as under the Confederation.

This Constitution, and the Laws of the United States which shall be made in Pursuance thereof; and all Treaties made, or which shall be made, under the Authority of the United States, shall be the supreme Law of the Land; and the Judges in every State shall be bound thereby, any Thing in the Constitution or Laws of any State to the Contrary notwithstanding.

The Senators and Representatives before mentioned, and the Members of the several State Legislatures, and all executive and judicial Officers, both of the United States and of the several States, shall be bound by Oath or Affirmation, to support this Constitution; but no religious Test shall ever be required as a Qualification to any Office or public Trust under the United States.

Article. VII.

The Ratification of the Conventions of nine States, shall be sufficient for the Establishment of this Constitution between the States so ratifying the Same.

The Word, "the," being interlined between the seventh and eighth Lines of the first Page, the Word "Thirty" being partly written on an Erazure in the fifteenth Line of the first Page, The Words "is tried" being interlined between the thirty second and thirty third Lines of the first Page and the Word "the" being interlined between the forty third and forty fourth Lines of the second Page.

Attest William Jackson Secretary

done in Convention by the Unanimous Consent of the States present the Seventeenth Day of September in the Year of our Lord one thousand seven hundred and Eighty seven and of the Independance of the United States of America the Twelfth In witness whereof We have hereunto subscribed our Names,

G°. Washington
Presidt and deputy from Virginia

Delaware
Geo: Read
Gunning Bedford jun
John Dickinson
Richard Bassett
Jaco: Broom

Maryland
James McHenry
Dan of St Thos. Jenifer
Danl. Carroll

Virginia
John Blair
James Madison Jr.

North Carolina
Wm. Blount
Richd. Dobbs Spaight
Hu Williamson

South Carolina
J. Rutledge
Charles Cotesworth
Pinckney
Charles Pinckney
Pierce Butler

Georgia
William Few
Abr Baldwin

New Hampshire
John Langdon
Nicholas Gilman

Massachusetts
Nathaniel Gorham
Rufus King

Connecticut
Wm. Saml. Johnson
Roger Sherman

New York
Alexander Hamilton

New Jersey
Wil: Livingston
David Brearley
Wm. Paterson
Jona: Dayton

Pennsylvania
B Franklin
Thomas Mifflin
Robt. Morris
Geo. Clymer
Thos. FitzSimons
Jared Ingersoll
James Wilson
Gouv Morris

BOOKS

Cheney, Lynne. *We the People: The Story of Our Constitution.* New York: Simon and Schuster Children's Publishing, 2008.

Ransom, Candice F. *George Washington and the Story of the U.S. Constitution.* Minneapolis, Minnesota: Lerner Classroom, 2011.

Ransom, Candice F. *Who Wrote the U.S. Constitution? And Other Questions About the Constitutional Convention of 1787.* Minneapolis, Minnesota: Lerner Classroom, 2010.

Taylor-Butler, Christine. *The Constitution of the United States.* New York: Scholastic Books, 2008.

Travis, Cathy. *The Constitution Translated for Kids.* Austin, Texas: Ovation Books, 2008.

Wyatt, Valerie. *How to Build Your Own Country.* Tonawanda, New York: Kids Can Press, 2009.

WORKS CONSULTED

Arnheim, Dr. Michael. *U.S. Constitution for Dummies.* Hoboken, New Jersey: Wiley Publishing, 2009.

Bowen, Catherine Drinker. *Miracle at Philadelphia.* Boston: Little, Brown, 1986.

Lomask, Milton. *The Spirit of 1787: The Making of Our Constitution.* New York: Farrar Straus Giroux, 1980.

National Archives: The Charters of Freedom
http://www.archives.gov/exhibits/charters/

Stevens, William. "Behind the Scenes in 1787: Secrecy in the Heat." *The New York Times,* May 25, 1987. http://www.nytimes.com/1987/05/25/us/behind-the-scenes-in-1787-secrecy-in-the-heat.html?src=pm

Teaching American History: The Constitutional Convention
http://teachingamericanhistory.org/convention/

ON THE INTERNET

Ben's Guide to the U.S. Government for Kids: The History of the Constitution
http://bensguide.gpo.gov/6-8/documents/constitution/background.html

Congress for Kids: Constitution
http://www.congressforkids.net/Constitution_delegates.htm

The Constitution
http://www.whitehouse.gov/our-government/the-constitution

amendment (uh-MEND-munt)—An official or formal change or addition to the Constitution.

anarchy (AN-ar-kee)—The state of lawlessness or disorder that results from having no government.

Anti-Federalist (an-ty-FEH-druh-list)—A person who was against or had serious concerns about accepting the Constitution.

bicameral (by-KAM-uh-rul)—Made up of two chambers or houses.

delegate (DEH-lih-git)—A person chosen to act or represent others.

export (EKS-port)—To ship a good to another country for sale or exchange.

Federalist (FEH-drul-ist)—A person who believed the Constitution should be accepted.

import (IM-port)—To bring in a product or resource from a foreign country for use or sale.

monarchy (MAH-nar-kee)—A state or nation ruled by a single person, such as a king or queen.

ratify (RAT-ih-fy)—To confirm by showing approval or consent.

representation (rep-ree-sen-TAY-shun)—Speaking on behalf of another person or group of people.

resolution (reh-zuh-LOO-shun)—A formal expression of an opinion or intention.

trade regulation (TRAYD reg-yoo-LAY-shun)—Laws regarding what can be bought and sold.

tyranny (TEER-uh-nee)—Government or rule by a tyrant or absolute ruler.

ABOUT THE
AUTHOR

Tamra Orr is a full-time author living in the Pacific Northwest with her family. She has written more than 250 nonfiction books for readers of all ages. She has a degree in English and Secondary Education from Ball State University. Orr's interest in the history of the Constitution began when she wrote a book about the Federalists in 2005. She also wrote a book about the Tenth Amendment and how it affects the United States. In her fifteen minutes of free time, she loves reading, writing letters, and looking at Oregon scenery.